The

MAJOR LEAGUE BASEBALL BOOK OF

Fabulous Facts

AND AWESOME TRIVIA

From the Legendary

to the Obscure,

Baseball Questions

Covering All the Numbers,

the Moments,

the Records,

Even the Nicknames

THE

MAJOR LEAGUE BASEBALL BOOK OF

Fabulous Facts

AND AWESOME TRIVIA

KEN SHOULER

Quill

A HarperResource Book

An Imprint of HarperCollins*Publishers*

HarperCollins books may be purchased for educational, business, or sales promotional use. For information please write: Special Markets Department, HarperCollins Publishers, Inc., 10 East 53rd Street, New York, NY 10022.

FIRST EDITION

Designed by Judith Stagnitto Abbate/Abbate Design

Library of Congress Cataloging-in-Publication Data has been applied for

ISBN 0-06-107373-3

04   05   RRD   10   9   8   7   6   5

Contents

Foreword

I N THE EYES of the right beholder, baseball trivia is an important pastime. Paradoxical but true—baseball trivia is significant. In other sports, trivia is as forced as a pass into a crowd. Try asking someone how many points Michael Jordan scored or how many yards Johnny Unitas passed for. Only a lifelong resident of Nerdville would know or care. The history of those games isn't nearly as celebrated as baseball history is. Two of the ineffable charms of baseball are its history and statistics, making it a far more intriguing subject for trivia.

My introduction to the serious pursuit of knowledge to be gleaned from trivia occurred fourteen summers ago at Runyons. At this Front Page–style restaurant on Second Avenue in New York City, a copy of *Total Baseball* was always within arm's reach of the corner table. Several of the habitués who liked to create trivia questions—Gene Orza, Terry Cashman, and Joe Healy, to name a few—made up a group that appeared on sports radio stations or the Madison Square Garden channel. I recall that sportscaster Dave Simms would sometimes moderate the contests. If you stumped this group—a Sisyphean task in itself—they'd quid pro quo you with a question of their own. The chance of finding a hole with your question, and then hitting their offering, was about the same chance as your softball team has of beating the New York Yankees. The probabilities were somewhere between slim and none, and Slim always seemed to be *just* leaving town.

Despite the infinitesimal odds, I did succeed against the Group on the radio one Opening Day. "Name two pitchers who won 20 games and had more wins than walks in those years," I commanded, knowing I'd thrown a high and tight one. No one knew. The two pitchers were Slim Sallee, a left-hander who won 21 with the 1919 Reds and walked just 20, and the Giants' great hurler, Christy Mathewson, who won 25 in 1913 and 25 in 1914 while walking just 21 and 23 in those years. I expected a return question about pitchers, since they liked to return fire with roughly similar fire. "What pitcher went 0 for 12 as a hitter one season?" Gene Orza asked. I remembered something I'd just read (on such chance occurrences our proudest trivia moments turn) about Koufax being an especially weak-hitting pitcher, so I blurted out, "Sandy Koufax." I was right (Koufax also went 0–26 two years later). The prize—a boom box, which I had to pick up at the radio station but never did—was secondary. I just enjoyed the small triumph of slipping a question by these guys, who really knew and loved the game, especially its numerical treasures.

If no answer to a question seemed imminent, they'd move the question along with hints. If the question was "Name the players with ten or more letters in their last names who hit 40 homers in season," you might get three in short order but get stalled on Rico Petrocelli. After thirty

Foreword

seconds of silence, a merciful hint followed: "American League infielder, 1960s." If you couldn't get the answer after that generous offering, you were out of luck.

They drew me into trivia and it always seemed like an entertaining way to skip across baseball history and statistics. Here's hoping it does the same for you.

—KEN SHOULER

CHAPTER 1

Baseball Starters

1. Who among the following had no part in "inventing" the modern game of baseball?

   a. Dr. Daniel Lucius Adams
   b. Abner Doubleday
   c. Alexander Cartwright

2. What team is acknowledged to be the first all-professional team?

3. Who was the first black Major League player, for the American Association Toledo Club, in 1884?

4. What team won in its first five World Series appearances?

   a. Boston (AL)
   b. Philadelphia (AL)
   c. Detroit (AL)

5. America's first professional baseball league was

    a. the National League
    b. the National Association
    c. the American League

6. Jackie Robinson signed a contract to play for Brooklyn's top farm team, Montreal, in what year?

7. The first National Association championship in 1871 was won by what team?

8. The first radio broadcast of a Major League baseball game occurred in what year, in what city, and on what station?

9. When was the first baseball game televised?

10. Name at least five Major League baseball players who appeared on American postage stamps before the year 2000.

1. b.

2. The Cincinnati Red Stockings in 1869

3. Moses Fleetwood Walker, a catcher

4. a. Boston won in 1903, 1912, 1915, 1916, 1918.

5. b. The National Association was created in 1871.

6. 1945

7. The Philadelphia Athletics

8. The first broadcast of a Major League game was on KDKA in Pittsburgh in 1921. The broadcaster was Harold Arlin.

9. The first game ever televised was on May 17, 1939. The game, between Princeton and Columbia, was seen by a handful of viewers via W2XBS in New York City.

10. Jim Thorpe, Babe Ruth, Lou Gehrig, Jackie Robinson, Roberto Clemente, Roger Maris

CHAPTER 2

Moments

1. Who hit the first walk-off home run in history to win a World Series?

2. In 1961 this player hit his sixty-first home run off what pitcher?

3. Did Mark McGwire hit his seventieth homer at home or away?

4. This player hit the first All-Star Game home run in what year?

5. Who hit the only walk-off homer to win a World Series when his team was trailing in the game?

6. What pitcher struck out five future Hall of Famers in succession in the 1934 All-Star Game?

7. What pitcher won 2 games to help his team win the 1918 World Series?

8. This hurler struck out fifteen Yankees in Game One of the 1963 World Series.

9. True or false: Don Larsen pitched a perfect game against the Dodgers in the 1955 World Series.

10. In baseball's fiftieth All-Star Game in 1979, this out-fielder's strong throw cut down Brian Downing at the plate and stymied an American League rally.

11. He dropped the third strike in what game to ignite a Yankee rally in the World Series?

12. He hit .333 in the 1909 World Series and outplayed American League rival Ty Cobb.

13. Who struck out Tony Lazzeri to halt a seventh-game rally and help the Cardinals win the 1926 World Series?

14. He hit 3 home runs in what game of the 1977 World Series?

15. Jackie Robinson made his Major League debut on what date?

16. On August 29, 1965, this slugger hit his seventeenth homer in one month to break a National League record.

17. In 1970 this slugger became the ninth member of the 500-homer club when he bashed his.

18. Who were the two managers in the 1951 Dodgers-Giants playoff?

19. What National League team won 26 games in a row?

20. This 500-homer club member hit a home run in his last time at bat in the Major Leagues.

21. In what city and what year was night baseball first played?

22. He caught Willie McCovey's line drive to end what World Series?

23. On April 27, 1983, he broke Walter Johnson's strike-out record.

24. Two pitchers, one in the National League and one in the American League, threw no-hitters on the same day in 1990.

25. This Minnesota Twins pitcher, traded for Chuck Knoblauch, tossed a no-hitter in 1999.

26. In September 1999, he became the first player to hit 60 homers in back-to-back seasons.

27. Who tossed the only perfect game of 1999?

28. He hit 2 homers in Game Three of the 1998 World Series to give New York a comeback victory.

29. Who made two astounding catches in Game Three of the 1969 World Series to preserve a Mets victory.

30. He hit a series-turning home run in the ninth inning of Game Five of the 1986 American League Championship Series.

31. What was the score before Bobby Thomson hit his game-ending "Shot Heard 'Round the World" in the 1951 playoffs?

32. Who hit the line drive in Game Seven on which Enos Slaughter scampered home with the winning run of the 1946 World Series?

33. Who was the pitcher when Babe Ruth hit the alleged "called shot" in the 1932 World Series?

34. On June 3, 1932, he became the first player of the twentieth century to hit 4 home runs in 1 game.

35. Against what team did Joe DiMaggio end his 56-game hitting streak in 1941?

36. Who threw the pitch that Hank Aaron hit for home run number 715?

37. What pitcher won 3 games in the 1968 World Series and beat Bob Gibson in the finale?

38. What player's over-the-shoulder catch in Game One turned the 1954 World Series?

39. His home run clinched the National League pennant in 1957.

40. Eight days before he announced his retirement in 1935, he hit 3 home runs in a game at Forbes Field.

41. This player-manager led the 1926 Cardinals to a World Series victory.

42. He made a running one-handed catch to shut down a Yankee rally in Game Seven of the 1955 World Series.

43. Who shut out the Yankees in that same game?

44. What Seattle player hit the ball that scored Ken Griffey, Jr., in Game Five of the 1995 divisional playoffs?

45. In 1892, Pud Galvin and Tim Keefe (both 300-game winners at the time) started a game against each other. The next time that two 300-game winners faced each other was June 28, 1986, when Cleveland played California. Who were these two pitchers?

46. What Baltimore pitcher won the clinching game against Seattle in the 1997 American League Division Series?

47. What Minnesota hurler won Game Seven of the 1987 World Series?

48. True or false: Oakland's Rollie Fingers saved all 4 games of the 1972 World Series.

49. True or False: St. Louis's Bob Gibson won all three of his starts in the 1964 World Series.

50. Who was the winning pitcher in Game Six of the 1975 World Series, sometimes called "the finest World Series game ever played"?

51. This player hit his six hundredth home run on September 22, 1969.

52. What pitcher once struck out ten consecutive batters?

53. Who was the pitcher who surrendered Bucky Dent's 3-run homer that put the Yankees ahead in the 1-game playoff with Boston?

54. What three brothers played in the same outfield on September 15, 1963?

55. In 1997, he became the first National League player since Hank Aaron in 1959 to get 400 total bases in a season.

56. This Yankee right-hander took a no-hitter and 2–1 lead into the ninth inning of Game Four of the 1947 World Series, only to lose the no-hitter and the game when pinch hitter Cookie Lavagetto lined a 2-run double.

57. This recent Hall of Famer lined the infamous "Pine Tar" home run off Goose Gossage in 1983.

58. He replaced Lou Gehrig at first base on May 2, 1939, ending Gehrig's streak at 2,130 consecutive games.

59. This infielder started a double play that helped end Joe DiMaggio's 56-game hitting streak.

60. He integrated the American League in 1947.

61. In his first two Major League starts in 1936, he struck out thirty-two batters, then went home to finish high school.

62. This midget, wearing the number 1/8, batted once for the St. Louis Browns in 1951.

63. Against what team did Babe Ruth hit his first Major League home run?

64. Name the three players on the 1973 Braves who hit 40 home runs apiece.

65. He became the sixth member of the 500-homer club by launching one off Stu Miller on May 14, 1967.

66. He hurled a perfect game on May 9, 1968, becoming the first American Leaguer to throw a regular season perfecto in forty-six years.

67. He hit a homer in Game Seven to help clinch the 1973 World Series.

68. This Hall of Fame hurler won Game Six to give Cleveland the 1948 World Series.

69. He belted 4 homers in a game for Cleveland in 1959.

70. These two sluggers became the tenth and eleventh members of the 500-homer club on August 10 and September 13, 1971, respectively.

71. In 1996 he joined Hank Aaron and Willie Mays as the only players with 500 homers and 3,000 hits.

72. When he struck out nineteen White Sox batters in 1997 he became the first pitcher ever to strike out nineteen twice in the same season.

73. He hit home runs in 8 consecutive games to tie the record set by Dale Long and tied by Don Mattingly.

74. These two players reached 3,000 hits during the 1992 season.

75. He was named playoff MVP in 1989 after Oakland beat Toronto in 5 games.

76. He hit safely in 39 consecutive games in 1987.

77. At the age of forty-six, he became the oldest pitcher ever to hurl a shutout and won his three hundredth game on the last day of the 1985 season.

Moments

78. He hit his five hundredth homer in 1984 to become the thirteenth player to reach the plateau.

79. This pitcher broke Herb Score's rookie strikeout record in 1984.

80. This reliever saved the "Pine Tar" game in 1983.

81. He became the fifteenth pitcher to win 300 games when he beat the Yankees in 1982.

82. Pitching against the Yankees, he earned win number 300 in August 1985.

83. On October 14, 1976, he hit the home run that clinched the American League pennant.

84. In a doubleheader sweep of the Braves, this player hit 5 homers and knocked in 13 runs on August 1, 1972.

85. This player stole 7 bases in two consecutive World Series.

86. On July 31, 1954, this slugger used a borrowed bat and hit 4 home runs and a double in 1 game, tying the homer mark and setting a 1-game mark for total bases.

87. On September 29, 1969, this Boston infielder hit his fortieth home run, a then-record for American League shortstops.

88. This Met, running illegally inside the first-base line, was hit by pitcher Pete Richert's throw, enabling the Mets to win Game Four of the 1969 World Series.

89. He was the first 30-game winner since Dizzy Dean.

90. On two days' rest, this pitcher beat the Twins, 2–0, to give the Dodgers their second World Championship in three years in 1965.

91. He struck out seventeen players in Game One of the 1968 World Series to establish a new Series record.

92. On July 14, 1967, he hit his five hundredth homer off Juan Marichal to become the seventh member of the 500-homer club.

93. For several decades he held the National League record for home runs until Willie Mays broke his record on May 4, 1966.

94. In 1937, this Negro Leagues slugger hit a ball that came within two feet of leaving Yankee Stadium. The blow is estimated at 580 feet.

95. This Detroit slugger set a new record for home runs in a month when, in August 1937, he hit his eighteenth to eclipse Babe Ruth's old mark.

96. In 1936 and 1937 this lefty notched 24 consecutive wins.

97. On September 17, 1931, this Boston outfielder set the record for doubles with 65. He finished the season with 67.

98. His streak of 68 innings without a walk ended on July 18, 1913.

99. This slugging first baseman, who held the record for 3-homer games, did it for the sixth and final time on September 15, 1950.

1. Pittsburgh's Bill Mazeroski, in the Game Seven of the 1960 World Series

2. Roger Maris hit it off Boston's Tracy Stallard.

3. At home, against Montreal

4. Babe Ruth in 1934

5. Joe Carter, against Philadelphia in 1993

6. Carl Hubbell struck out Babe Ruth, Lou Gehrig, Jimmie Foxx, Al Simmons, and Joe Cronin in the first and second innings.

7. Babe Ruth, who was pitching for Boston, won 2.

8. Sandy Koufax

9. False. It was the 1956 World Series.

10. Dave Parker

11. Mickey Owen dropped it in Game Four of the 1941 World Series.

12. Pittsburgh shortstop Honus Wagner

13. Grover Cleveland Alexander

14. Reggie Jackson hit 3 in Game Six.

15. April 15, 1947

16. Willie Mays

17. Ernie Banks

18. Leo Durocher for the Giants and Chuck Dressen for the Dodgers

19. The New York Giants in 1916

20. Ted Williams

21. Cincinnati in 1935

22. Second baseman Bobby Richardson caught it in 1962.

23. Nolan Ryan struck out Brad Mills for strikeout number 3,510.

24. Oakland's Dave Stewart and Los Angeles' Fernando Valenzuela

25. Eric Milton

26. Sammy Sosa

27. David Cone

28. Scott Brosius

29. Tommy Agee

30. Boston's Dave Henderson

31. Brooklyn was ahead of New York, 4–2.

32. Harry "the Hat" Walker

33. Charlie Root

34. Lou Gehrig

35. The Cleveland Indians

36. Al Downing

37. Mickey Lolich

38. Willie Mays

39. Milwaukee's Hank Aaron

40. Babe Ruth

41. Rogers Hornsby

42. Sandy Amoros

43. Johnny Podres

44. Edgar Martinez

45. Don Sutton (301 wins, then with California) faced Phil Niekro (304 wins, then with Cleveland). Neither pitcher got a decision.

46. Mike Mussina

47. Frank Viola

48. False. He saved 2 games versus the Reds.

49. False. He lost his first start against New York and won the next two.

50. Boston's Rick Wise

51. Willie Mays

52. Tom Seaver struck out the last ten batters of a game against the San Diego Padres in 1970.

53. Mike Torrez

54. Felipe, Matty, and Jesus Alou played together in the Giants outfield for one inning. The Giants "benched" Willie Mays in the 13–5 victory.

55. Larry Walker

56. Bill Bevens

57. George Brett

58. Babe Dahlgren

59. Lou Boudreau

60. Larry Doby

61. Bob Feller

62. Eddie Gaedel

63. The New York Yankees, on May 6, 1915, at the Polo Grounds, for the Red Sox

64. Davey Johnson, with 43; Darrell Evans, with 41; Hank Aaron, with 40

65. Mickey Mantle

66. Jim "Catfish" Hunter

67. Reggie Jackson

68. Bob Lemon

69. Rocky Colavito

70. Harmon Killebrew and Frank Robinson

71. Eddie Murray

72. Randy Johnson

Moments

The Major League Baseball Book of Fabulous Facts and Awesome Trivia

76. Paul Molitor

77. Phil Niekro

78. Reggie Jackson

79. Dwight Gooden

80. Dan Quisenberry

81. Gaylord Perry

82. Tom Seaver

83. Chris Chambliss

84. Nate Colbert

85. Lou Brock did it in 1967 and 1968.

86. Joe Adcock

87. Rico Petrocelli

88. J. C. Martin

89. Denny McLain

90. Sandy Koufax

91. Bob Gibson

92. Eddie Mathews

93. Mel Ott

94. Josh Gibson

95. Rudy York

96. Carl Hubbell

97. Earl Webb

98. Christy Mathewson

99. Johnny Mize

CHAPTER 3

Numbers

1. At each position on the diamond there has been at least one player who won back-to-back MVP awards. Name at least one player at each position who has done this.

2. Eight infielders playing at first, shortstop, and third have hit 500 home runs. Name them.

3. Who is the only player to be in three consecutive World Series on three different teams?

4. True or false: The 111 wins posted by the 1954 Cleveland Indians were the most ever by an American League team in the 154-game era.

5. True or false: The New York Yankees' 114 wins in 1998 were the most ever by a Major League team.

6. Which of the following players has won the most slugging average titles?

   a. Ken Griffey, Jr.
   b. Mark McGwire
   c. Sammy Sosa

7. What four teams have won in their last three World Series appearances?

8. What two pitchers are tied with 373 wins?

9. Before wearing number 44, what number did Hank Aaron wear?

10. Who is the only player to win the Cy Young and Rookie of the Year Awards in the same season?

11. Who played 500 or more games at four different positions?

12. Who won more batting titles than any player in baseball history?

13. What pitcher has thrown the most complete games?

Numbers

14. This player had 200 hits and 100 walks in the same season for a record seven times in his career.

15. Three players share the record for most 100-RBI seasons, two of whom share the record for most consecutive 100-RBI seasons. Who are they and how many 100-RBI seasons do they have?

16. Name the players in baseball history who have had back-to-back 50-homer seasons.

17. Who averaged .402 for the five-year period from 1921 through 1925?

18. He is the only shortstop who passed 400 home runs, 1,500 runs batted in, and 3,000 hits.

19. Name the two players tied with a record sixteen Gold Gloves.

20. Who played on a winning World Series team more times than any player in baseball history?

21. What Hall of Fame catchers won three MVPs each?

22. What slugger led the 1960s in home runs?

23. He was the first player ever to hit 400 home runs and collect 3,000 hits.

24. Who holds the record for winning the home run title for the most consecutive seasons?

25. Who led the National League in stolen bases for four consecutive seasons from 1956 through 1959?

26. He has the record for most RBIs in one season.

27. Who holds the record for the highest single-season batting average in this century?

28. Who led the National League in slugging average six times before the "live ball era" even began?

29. Name the outfielder who led the American League in slugging average eight times in the "dead ball era."

30. Who won more games than any left-hander in Major League history?

31. What pitcher posted a 79–15 record in one three-year period?

32. What was the distance of the center field fence in Yankee Stadium in the year the park opened?

33. What World Series–winning team had the worst regular season record?

34. What National League team was the first to draw two million paying customers at home?

35. He led the league in wins more than any other pitcher in the history of baseball. Who is he?

36. What was the last year the Washington Senators played?

37. This franchise has gone the longest without winning a World Series.

38. What slugger led the 1930s in home runs?

39. What catcher for the Chicago Cubs was also a pocket billiards world champion in 1909?

40. What Major League baseball teams did Jim Thorpe play for?

41. What Major League team and in what year did the *Field of Dreams* character Moonlight Graham really play for?

42. What batter holds the dubious record for striking out the most times in a season?

43. Who won the first Cy Young Award—given for both leagues—in 1956?

44. What Yankee, besides Babe Ruth, led the American League in home runs in the 1920s?

45. When Steve Carlton won 27 games in 1972, how many games did his team win?

46. True or false: Before Greg Maddux, the last player to win back-to-back ERA titles was Ron Guidry.

47. True or false: Elmer Flick's .308 batting average for Cleveland in 1905 was the lowest to lead the league in American League history.

48. True or false: Just one Yankee has won the Cy Young Award since Whitey Ford won it in 1961.

49. Name the four Dodgers to win consecutive Rookie of the Year Awards from 1979 to 1982.

50. What pitcher had a record of 18–1 in 1959?

1. Pitcher, Hal Newhouser; catcher, Yogi Berra; first base, Jimmie Foxx, Frank Thomas; second base, Joe Morgan; shortstop, Ernie Banks; third base, Mike Schmidt; outfield, Roger Maris, Mickey Mantle, Dale Murphy, Barry Bonds

2. Jimmie Foxx, Harmon Killebrew, Willie McCovey, Mark McGwire, Eddie Murray, Ernie Banks, Mike Schmidt, Eddie Mathews

3. Don Baylor from 1986 through 1988

4. True

5. False. The 1906 Chicago Cubs won 116 games.

6. b. Mark McGwire has won four slugging titles; Griffey, one; Sosa, none.

7. The Yankees, Tigers, Reds, Pirates

8. Grover Cleveland Alexander and Christy Mathewson

9. Number 5.

10. Fernando Valenzuela, in 1981

11. Pete Rose

12. Ty Cobb. He won twelve of the thirteen batting titles between 1907 and 1919.

13. Cy Young, with 749

14. Lou Gehrig

15. Babe Ruth, Lou Gehrig, and Jimmie Foxx each had thirteen 100-RBI seasons. Gehrig and Foxx had thirteen consecutive 100-RBI seasons.

16. Babe Ruth, Mark McGwire (four consecutive), Sammy Sosa, Ken Griffey, Jr.

17. Rogers Hornsby, with 1,078 hits in 2,679 at bats for a .4024 average

18. Cal Ripken

19. Brooks Robinson and Jim Kaat

20. Yogi Berra, ten times

21. Yogi Berra and Roy Campanella

22. Harmon Killebrew

23. Stan Musial

24. Ralph Kiner, seven times from 1946 through 1952

25. Willie Mays

26. Hack Wilson had 191 in 1930.

27. Rogers Hornsby, who hit .424 in 1924

28. Honus Wagner

The Major League Baseball Book of Fabulous Facts and Awesome Trivia

29. Ty Cobb

30. Warren Spahn, with 363 games

31. Lefty Grove, 1929 through 1931

32. 490 feet in 1923

33. The 1987 Minnesota Twins, 85–77

34. In 1954 Milwaukee drew 2,131,388 fans.

35. Warren Spahn, eight times

36. 1971

37. The Chicago Cubs, ninety-one years

38. Jimmie Foxx, with 415

39. Johnny Kling

40. The New York Giants, 1913–1915; Cincinnati, 1917;
New York Giants, 1917–1919; Boston Braves, 1919

41. Archibald "Moonlight" Graham played 1 game for the New York Giants in 1905.

42. Bobby Bonds, 189 times in 1970

43. Brooklyn pitcher Don Newcombe

44. Bob Meusel led in 1925.

45. The Phillies won 59 games.

46. False. Roger Clemens did it from 1990 through 1992.

47. False. Carl Yastrzemski hit .3005 in 1968.

48. False. Sparky Lyle won the award in 1977, and Ron Guidry won it in 1978.

49. Rick Sutcliffe, Steve Howe, Fernando Valenzuela, Steve Sax

50. Elroy Face of the Pirates

CHAPTER 4

Teams

Anaheim Angels

1. Which Angels manager has won the most games?

2. Who was the first and only Cy Young Award winner for the Angels?

3. What two Hall of Famers' numbers did the Angels retire?

4. What was the first park that the Angels ever played in?

5. True or false: The Angels have played in one World Series.

6. Who was the Angels' only MVP award winner?

BALTIMORE ORIOLES

7. Name three of the Orioles' four Cy Young Award winners.

8. Name three of the Orioles' four MVP winners.

9. What was the first year in which there was an American League team named the Baltimore Orioles?

10. What team did the modern Orioles replace?

11. How many times have the Orioles made the World Series?

12. What numbers have the Orioles retired?

BOSTON RED SOX

13. What Boston Red Sox manager was the only one to win more than 1,000 games with the franchise?

14. How many World Series have the Red Sox been in since their last Series win in 1918?

15. Name five of the nine Red Sox ever to win an MVP award.

16. Name three of the four Red Sox who had their uniform numbers retired.

17. Name the last Boston player to win the home run title.

18. Name the last Red Sox player to win a batting title.

CHICAGO WHITE SOX

19. Who is the only White Sox player ever to win back-to-back MVP awards?

20. What was the last season the White Sox won a World Series?

21. Name the team they defeated in that World Series.

22. How many times have the White Sox played in the World Series?

23. True or false: The Chicago Cubs and the Chicago White Sox have never met in the World Series.

24. Which White Sox pitcher has won the most games?

CLEVELAND INDIANS

25. True or false: Manny Ramirez set a team record for RBIs in 1999.

26. What Cleveland manager led the Indians to 111 wins in 1954?

27. What was the name of the first stadium the Indians played in from 1901 through 1909?

28. Name the last Cleveland player to win the homer title.

29. What Cleveland hurler led the league in strikeouts seven times?

30. He was the last Indian hurler to win more than 20 games.

DETROIT TIGERS

31. Who was the Tigers' last 20-game winner?

32. Who was the last Tiger to win a Cy Young Award?

33. True or false: The Tigers have won the last four World Series they have participated in.

34. Name the last Tiger to win an MVP award.

35. How many World Series have the Tigers won?

36. True or false: Denny McLain was the only 30-game winner in Tigers history.

KANSAS CITY ROYALS

37. In what year did the Kansas City Royals begin play?

38. True or false: The Royals have played in the World Series three times.

39. True or false: Of the fifteen Major League expansion teams since 1961, the Royals have the best all-time won-loss record.

40. Who is the Royals' only MVP winner?

41. Two Royals pitchers have won Cy Young Awards. Who are they?

42. Besides George Brett, what other Royals player has won a batting title?

MINNESOTA TWINS

43. What franchise shifted to Minnesota in 1960 when the Twins began?

44. What was the name of the Twins' home park before the current Hubert H. Humphrey Metrodome?

45. Name the three Twins MVPs.

46. Name Minnesota's two Cy Young Award winners.

47. Who is the Twins' all-time leader in batting average?

48. Who is the Twins' all-time home run leader?

New York Yankees

49. Before they were the Yankees, what was New York's team name?

50. Name the three managers to win more than 1,000 games with the Yankees.

51. In what year did the Yankees win their first World Series?

52. In what decade did the Yankees win the most World Series?

53. How many pennants have the Yankees won?

54. The Yankees have had twelve different MVP winners. Name nine of them.

OAKLAND ATHLETICS

55. In what year did the A's make their debut in Oakland?

56. Name six of the A's eleven MVP winners.

57. What Philadelphia A's legend won more than 3,500 games as a manager?

58. Name the last A's pitcher to win 20 games.

59. Who are the two A's left-handed pitchers who combined for thirteen strikeout titles?

60. What four active players won Rookie of the Year Awards with Oakland?

SEATTLE MARINERS

61. True or false: Seattle has gone to the World Series only once.

62. True or false: The Mariners have had one Rookie of the Year since their beginning in 1977.

63. Name the most recent Mariner to win a batting title.

64. How many home run titles has Ken Griffey, Jr., won?

65. Who is the Mariners' career batting leader?

66. What hurler is Seattle's career leader in wins?

TAMPA BAY DEVIL RAYS

67. In what year did the Devil Rays begin?

68. What Tampa Bay third baseman reached 3,000 hits in 1999?

69. Who hit the most homers for Tampa Bay in 1999?

70. Who led Tampa Bay in batting in 1999?

71. What is the name of the stadium where Tampa Bay plays?

72. Who led Tampa Bay in saves in 1999?

TEXAS RANGERS

73. What team relocated to Arlington to become the Texas Rangers?

74. How many years has Texas reached the postseason?

75. What pitcher has won more games than any other Texas pitcher?

76. Name Texas' three MVP winners.

77. True or false: No Texas pitcher has won a Cy Young Award.

78. True or false: The only Texas pitcher to hurl a no-hitter was Nolan Ryan.

TORONTO BLUE JAYS

79. What year did the Blue Jays begin play?

80. Name the players who won the Sport Magazine Award (for World Series MVP) for Toronto in 1992 and 1993.

Teams

81. True or false: Toronto is one of two teams to surpass four million in annual attendance.

82. Name the only Blue Jays player to win the MVP award.

83. Name the last Blue Jays player to win the Cy Young Award.

84. Who is Toronto's all-time leader in batting average?

ARIZONA DIAMONDBACKS

85. What is the name of the ballpark Arizona plays in?

86. Has any expansion team made it to the postseason as quickly as Arizona?

87. Who led Arizona in batting in 1999?

88. What pitcher led Arizona in wins in 1999?

89. True or false: Arizona's leader in home runs in 1999 was Matt Williams.

90. True or false: The 1999 season was Arizona's first above .500.

ATLANTA BRAVES

91. Before Atlanta, what two cities did the Braves play in?

92. Who led the Braves in batting in 1999?

93. In what years did the Braves win the World Series?

94. Name four of the five Braves whose numbers have been retired.

95. Six different Braves have won MVPs. Name three of them.

96. What two players are tied for most homers in a season for the Braves?

CHICAGO CUBS

97. This manager had more victories than any Cubs skipper in the twentieth century.

Teams

98. How many pennants did the Cubs win last century?

99. How many World Series have the Cubs won?

100. Who was the last Cub to win a batting title?

101. Name five of the Cubs' nine MVP winners.

102. What two Cubs managers won the Manager of the Year award in the 1980s?

CINCINNATI REDS

103. Before playing in Riverfront Stadium, the Reds played in what park?

104. Nine different Reds players have won MVPs. Name six of them.

105. Who was the last Reds pitcher to win 20 games?

106. Who led the Reds in home runs in 1999?

107. He was the last Reds player to lead the league in batting.

108. He had more career wins than any other Reds pitcher.

COLORADO ROCKIES

109. True or false: Colorado finished above .500 in just its third year in the National League.

110. Name the first stadium where the Rockies played.

111. What three Colorado players have won the slugging title?

112. In what year did the Rockies draw the most fans?

113. What is the Rockies' record in the postseason?

114. He has the Colorado record for home runs in a season.

FLORIDA MARLINS

115. True or false: The Marlins won a World Series faster than any other expansion team has.

116. Name Florida's first manager.

117. Who was Florida's winning pitcher in the seventh game of the 1997 World Series?

118. Name the Marlins' MVP of the 1997 World Series.

119. True or false: Before their World Series victory, the Marlins had never finished a season with a better than .500 record.

120. What Florida player had the game-winning hit in the seventh game of the 1997 World Series victory against Cleveland?

HOUSTON ASTROS

121. Name Houston's first manager.

122. Who is the only Astro ever to win an MVP award?

123. Before they were the Astros, what were the Houston players called?

124. Who led the Astros in hitting in 1999?

125. True or false: Houston has appeared in one World Series.

126. Which pitcher has won the most games in Astros' history?

LOS ANGELES DODGERS

127. Name four of the Dodgers' six different Cy Young winners.

128. Three Dodgers managers have won more than 1,000 games. Who are they?

129. Before they moved into Dodger Stadium in 1962, what stadium did the Dodgers play in?

130. True or false: Next to the Yankees, the Dodgers won more pennants last century than any other team.

131. Who led the Dodgers in hitting in 1999?

132. What Dodger won more than one MVP?

MILWAUKEE BREWERS

133. What American League team became the Milwaukee Brewers?

134. Who are the two Brewers MVPs?

135. Who are the Brewers' two Cy Young Award winners?

136. Name two of the three Brewers to win American League home run titles.

137. This All-Star led the Brewers in homers in 1999.

138. What Brewer had a record 5 for 5 in Game One of the 1982 World Series?

MONTREAL EXPOS

139. This player hit more home runs as an Expo than any other player in their history.

140. What 1980s pitcher is the Expos' all-time winner as a pitcher?

141. He is the only Expo pitcher ever to win 20 games.

142. He was the last Expo to throw a no-hitter.

143. Who holds the all-time Expo record for RBIs in a season?

144. What future three-time Cy Young Award winner and which World Series MVP played for the 1994 Expos?

Teams

NEW YORK METS

145. Name the two Mets pitchers who have won Cy Young Awards.

146. Where did the Mets play before playing in Shea Stadium?

147. This former Met is the team's all-time leader in stolen bases.

148. He has more wins than any pitcher in Mets history.

149. What Met player started the winning rally with a single in Game Six of the 1986 World Series?

150. Who was the Mets MVP of the 1969 World Series?

PHILADELPHIA PHILLIES

151. This Phillies manager of the sixties won more games than any other Philadelphia skipper has won.

152. Who was the last Phillies player to win a batting title?

153. Name the three different Philadelphia hurlers who have won Cy Young Awards since 1972.

154. Four Hall of Famers have had their numbers retired by the Phillies. Who are they?

155. How many times did Hall of Famer Mike Schmidt lead the league in home runs?

156. He was the only Philadelphia pitcher to throw a perfect game.

PITTSBURGH PIRATES

157. The Pirates won two of their five World Series against which team?

158. Who was the most recent Pirates player to have his number retired?

159. Six different Pirates have won MVPs. Name four.

160. He was the last Pirate to win the homer and RBI championships.

Teams

161. Before the area beyond the left field fence in Forbes Field was named Kiner's Korner it was named what?

162. He was the last Pirate to win a batting title.

ST. LOUIS CARDINALS

163. The St. Louis Cardinals have won how many World Series?

164. The Cardinals won most of their World Series in what decade?

165. Before they played in Busch Memorial Stadium, the Cardinals played in what park?

166. He won three MVPs, more than any other Cardinal player.

167. He was the last Cardinal to win an MVP.

168. Eight Cardinal players have had their numbers retired. Name five.

SAN DIEGO PADRES

169. This San Diego pitcher led the team in wins in 1999.

170. Name one of the two Padres players who have had their numbers retired.

171. Tony Gwynn won eight batting titles. Who is the only other Padres player to win one?

172. True or false: The Padres have appeared in two World Series.

173. Name the Padre who led the team in hits in the 1998 World Series.

174. This Padre is their all-time leader in wins.

SAN FRANCISCO GIANTS

175. What team did the Giants beat in two consecutive World Series?

Teams

176. What Giants skipper managed them to more than 2,500 wins?

177. Who has the Giants' highest slugging average in a season?

178. Before moving into Candlestick Park in 1960, the Giants played in this park.

179. Name six of the seven Giants players whose uniform numbers were retired.

180. Six different Giants have won MVPs. Name four of them.

1. Bill Rigney won 625 games from 1961 through 1969.

2. Dean Chance in 1964

3. Rod Carew (29) and Nolan Ryan (30)

4. Wrigley Field in Los Angeles in 1961

5. False. The Angels have not appeared in a World Series.

6. Don Baylor in 1979

7. Mike Cuellar, in 1969, tied with Denny McLain; Jim Palmer, in 1973, 1975, 1976; Mike Flanagan, in 1979; Steve Stone, in 1980

8. Brooks Robinson, in 1964; Frank Robinson, in 1966; Boog Powell, in 1970; Cal Ripken, in 1983, 1991

9. 1901

10. In 1954 the Orioles replaced the St. Louis Browns.

11. Six times: in 1966, 1969, 1970, 1971, 1979, 1983

12. Earl Weaver (4), Brooks Robinson (5), Frank Robinson (20), Jim Palmer (22), Eddie Murray (33)

13. Joe Cronin won 1,071 from 1935 through 1947.

14. Four: the 1946, 1967, 1975, and 1986 World Series

15. Tris Speaker, in 1912; Jimmie Foxx, in 1938; Ted Williams, in 1946, 1949; Jackie Jensen, in 1958; Carl Yastrzemski, in 1967; Fred Lynn, in 1975; Jim Rice, in 1978; Roger Clemens, in 1986; Mo Vaughn, in 1995

16. Bobby Doerr (1), Joe Cronin (4), Carl Yastrzemski (8), Ted Williams (9)

17. Tony Armas, in 1984

18. Nomar Garciaparra, in 2000

19. Frank Thomas, in 1993 and 1994

20. 1917

21. They beat the New York Giants, 4–2.

22. Four: in 1906, 1917, 1919, 1959

23. False. The two teams played in 1906 and the White Sox won.

24. Ted Lyons, with 260

25. True. Ramirez had 165. The previous record was Hal Trosky with 162 in 1936.

26. Al Lopez

27. League Park

28. Albert Belle in 1995

29. Bob Feller

30. Gaylord Perry was 21–13 in 1974.

31. Bill Gullickson won 20 in 1991.

32. Willie Hernandez, in 1984

33. False. They won in 1984, 1968, 1945, but lost to Cincinnati in 1940.

34. Willie Hernandez, in 1984

35. Four: in 1935, 1945, 1968, 1984

36. True. Lady Baldwin won 42 for Detroit when they were the National League Wolverines in 1886. Pete Conway won 30 for the Wolverines in 1888.

37. 1969

38. False. They played in the World Series twice, in 1980 and 1985.

39. False. They have won 2548 and lost 2497 through 2000 (.505), but the Arizona Diamondbacks have won 250 and lost 236 (.514) over the same time.

40. George Brett, in 1980

41. Bret Saberhagen, in 1985, 1989; David Cone, in 1994

42. Willie Wilson, who hit .332 in 1982

43. The Washington Senators

44. Metropolitan Stadium, where they played from 1961 through 1981

45. Zoilo Versailles, in 1965; Harmon Killebrew, in 1969; Rod Carew, in 1977

46. Jim Perry, in 1970; Frank Viola, in 1988

47. Rod Carew, who hit .334 in a Twins uniform

48. Harmon Killebrew, with 573

49. The Highlanders

50. Miller Huggins, with 1,067; Joe McCarthy, with 1,460; Casey Stengel, with 1,149

51. 1923

52. They won six in the 1950s.

53. 37

54. Babe Ruth, in 1923; Lou Gehrig, in 1927, 1936; Joe DiMaggio, in 1939, 1941, 1949; Joe Gordon, in 1942; Spud Chandler, in 1943; Phil Rizzuto, in 1950; Yogi Berra, in 1951, 1954, 1955; Mickey Mantle, in 1956, 1957, 1962; Roger Maris, in 1960, 1961; Elston Howard, in 1963; Thurman Munson, in 1976; Don Mattingly, in 1985

55. 1968

56. In Philadelphia: Eddie Collins, in 1914; Mickey Cochrane, in 1928; Lefty Grove, in 1931; Jimmie Foxx in, 1932, 1933; Bobby Shantz, in 1953; in Oakland: Vida Blue, in 1971; Reggie Jackson, in 1973; Jose Canseco, in 1988; Rickey Henderson, in 1990; Dennis Eckersley, in 1992; Jason Giambi, in 2000

57. Connie Mack won 3,582 games from 1901 through 1950.

58. Bob Welch won 27 in 1990.

59. Rube Waddell and Lefty Grove

60. Jose Canseco, in 1986; Mark McGwire, in 1987; Walt Weiss, in 1988; Ben Grieve, in 1998

61. False. It has never gone to the Series.

62. False. Alvin Davis won the award in 1984, and Kazuhiro Sasaki won in 2000.

63. Alex Rodriguez hit .358 in 1996.

64. Four.

65. Edgar Martinez has hit .320 for Seattle.

66. Randy Johnson won 130 games with Seattle.

67. 1998

68. Wade Boggs

69. Jose Canseco hit 34.

70. Fred McGriff hit .310.

71. The Thunderdome

72. Roberto Hernandez saved 43 games.

73. The Washington Senators, in 1972

74. Three: 1996, 1998, 1999

75. Charlie Hough won 139.

76. Jeff Burroughs, in 1974; Juan Gonzalez, in 1996,
1998; Ivan Rodriguez, in 1999.

77. True

78. False. Jim Bibby did it in 1973; Bert Blyleven in 1977; Nolan Ryan in 1990, 1991; Kenny Rogers in 1994.

79. 1977

80. Pat Borders, in 1992; Paul Molitor, in 1993

81. True. It surpassed four million in 1991, 1992, and 1993.

82. Jorge Bell (also known as George Bell), in 1987

83. Roger Clemens, in 1998

84. Roberto Alomar, .307

85. Bank One Ballpark

86. No. Arizona made it in its second year.

87. Luis Gonzalez hit .336.

88. Randy Johnson won 17 games.

89. False. Jay Bell hit 38; Matt Williams hit 35.

90. True

91. Boston and Milwaukee

92. Chipper Jones hit .319.

93. 1914, 1957, 1995

94. Dale Murphy (3), Warren Spahn (21), Phil Niekro (35), Ed Mathews (41), Hank Aaron (44)

95. Johnny Evers, in 1914; Bob Elliott, in 1947; Hank Aaron, in 1957; Dale Murphy, in 1982, 1983; Terry Pendleton, in 1991; Chipper Jones, in 1999

96. Eddie Mathews, in 1953, and Hank Aaron, in 1971, both hit 47 in a season.

97. Charlie Grimm won 946 games with the Cubs in 1932–1938, 1944–1949, and 1960.

The Major League Baseball Book of Fabulous Facts and Awesome Trivia

98. Ten

99. Two

100. Bill Buckner hit .324 in 1980.

101. Wildfire Schulte, in 1911; Rogers Hornsby, in 1929; Gabby Hartnett, in 1935; Phil Cavarretta, in 1945; Hank Sauer, in 1952; Ernie Banks, in 1958, 1959; Ryne Sandberg, in 1984; Andre Dawson, in 1987; Sammy Sosa, in 1998

102. Jim Frey, in 1984; Don Zimmer in 1989

103. Crosley Field, from 1912 through 1969

104. Ernie Lombardi, in 1938; Bucky Walters, in 1939; Frank McCormick, in 1940; Frank Robinson, in 1961; Johnny Bench, in 1970, 1972; Pete Rose, in 1973; Joe Morgan, in 1975, 1976; George Foster, in 1977; Barry Larkin, in 1995

105. Danny Jackson won 23 in 1988.

106. Greg Vaughn hit 45.

107. Pete Rose hit .338 in 1973.

108. Eppa Rixey won 179 games.

109. True

110. Mile High Stadium

111. Dante Bichette slugged .620 in 1995, Ellis Burks .639 in 1996, and Larry Walker won the slugging title twice with .720 in 1997 and .710 in 1999.

112. In 1993, their first season, they drew 4,483,350 fans, a Major League record.

113. One win and 3 losses against the Braves in 1995

114. Larry Walker hit 49 in 1997.

115. True. They won in 1997, their fifth season.

116. Rene Lachemann managed from 1993 through 1996.

117. Jay Powell

118. Livan Hernandez

119. True

120. Edgar Renteria

121. Harry Craft, who managed from 1962 to 1964

122. Jeff Bagwell, in 1994

123. The Colt .45s

124. Carl Everett hit .325.

125. False. The Astros have not reached the World Series.

126. Joe Niekro won 144.

127. Don Newcombe, in 1956; Don Drysdale, in 1962; Sandy Koufax, in 1963, 1965, 1966; Mike Marshall, in 1974; Fernando Valenzuela, in 1981; Orel Hershiser, in 1988

128. Wilbert Robinson won 1,375 in 1914–1931; Walt
Alston won 2,040 in 1954–1976; and Tommy
Lasorda won 1,599 in 1976–1996.

129. They played in the Los Angeles Memorial Coliseum
from 1958 through 1961.

130. True. They won nineteen pennants last century.

131. Mark Grudzielanek hit .326 in 1999.

132. Roy Campanella won in 1951, 1953, and 1955.

133. The Seattle Pilots, in 1970

134. Rollie Fingers, in 1981; Robin Yount, in 1982, 1989

135. Rollie Fingers, in 1981; Pete Vuckovich, in 1982

136. George Scott, in 1975; Gorman Thomas, in 1979,
1982; Ben Oglivie, in 1980

137. Jeromy Burnitz hit 33.

138. Paul Molitor

139. Andre Dawson hit 225.

140. Steve Rogers, with 158 wins

141. Ross Grimsley won 20 in 1978.

142. Dennis Martinez, in 1991

143. Vladimir Guerrero, with 131 RBIs in 1999

144. Pedro Martinez and John Wetteland

145. Tom Seaver, in 1969, 1973, 1975; Dwight Gooden, in 1985

146. They played in the Polo Grounds in 1962 and 1963.

147. Mookie Wilson stole 281 bases.

148. Tom Seaver won 198 games with the Mets.

149. Gary Carter

150. Donn Clendenon

151. Gene Mauch won 646 games.

152. Richie Ashburn hit .350 in 1958.

153. Steve Carlton, in 1972, 1977, 1980, 1982; John Denny, in 1983; Steve Bedrosian, in 1987

154. Richie Ashburn (1), Mike Schmidt (20), Steve Carlton (32), Robin Roberts (36)

155. Mike Schmidt led the National League in home runs eight times.

156. Jim Bunning

157. The Baltimore Orioles

158. Willie Stargell (8)

159. Paul Waner, in 1927; Dick Groat, in 1960; Roberto Clemente, in 1966; Dave Parker, in 1978; Willie Stargell, in 1979; Barry Bonds, in 1990, 1992

160. Willie Stargell hit 44 home runs and knocked in 119 runs in 1973.

161. Greenberg Gardens

162. Bill Madlock hit .323 in 1983.

163. Nine

164. The 1940s: in 1942, 1944, and 1946

165. Sportsman's Park, from 1920 through 1966

166. Stan Musial, in 1943, 1946, 1948

167. Willie McGee, in 1985

168. Ozzie Smith (1), Red Schoendienst (2), Stan Musial
(6), Enos Slaughter (9), Ken Boyer (14), Dizzy Dean
(17), Lou Brock (20), Bob Gibson (45)

169. Andy Ashby

170. Steve Garvey (6) and Randy Jones (35)

171. Gary Sheffield, in 1992

172. True. In 1984 and 1998

173. Tony Gwynn

174. Eric Show won 100 games as a Padre.

175. They beat the Yankees in the 1921 and 1922 World Series.

176. John McGraw won 2,583 games for New York from 1902 through 1932.

177. In 1993 Barry Bonds slugged .677.

178. Seals Stadium in San Francisco, in 1958–1959

179. Bill Terry (3), Mel Ott (4), Carl Hubbell (11), Willie Mays (24), Juan Marichal (27), Willie McCovey (44), Orlando Cepeda (30)

180. Carl Hubbell, in 1933, 1936; Willie Mays, in 1954, 1965; Willie McCovey, in 1969; Kevin Mitchell, in 1989; Barry Bonds, in 1993; Jeff Kent, in 2000

CHAPTER 5

Immortal Records

1. Name the two players who stayed twenty-three years with one club.

2. Name three of the four pitchers who played twenty-five or more years.

3. What two moundsmen pitched a record twenty-one years with one club?

4. Who is the all-time leader in games played?

5. Cal Ripken ended his consecutive games streak at how many?

6. Name the three players (who played 1,000 or more games) with career averages of .350 or above.

7. In 1968 this slugger hit 10 homers in 20 at bats.

The Major League Baseball Book of Fabulous Facts and Awesome Trivia

8. These two players are tied for the National League record for leading the league in average.

9. What player batted .300 or above twenty-three years in a row?

10. The 1986 Cincinnati Reds had five players on their roster with 2,000 or more career hits. Name four of them.

11. Who has had more at bats than any player in baseball history?

12. Who holds the National League record for playing in consecutive games?

13. What team won the first World Series ever played?

14. What team has won the most World Series?

15. Since expansion baseball began in 1961, what team has won the most World Series?

16. What National League hitter led the Major Leagues in home runs in the 1970s?

17. True or false: When Tony Gwynn hit .370 in 1987, he posted the highest National League average since Rogers Hornsby.

18. Five Hall of Famers have averaged more than 30 home runs per season, more than 100 RBIs per season, and have better than .300 batting averages. Who are they?

19. True or false: The last National League player to bat .400 was Rogers Hornsby.

20. Who was the last National League hurler to pitch 300 innings in a season?

21. Who had the highest batting average of any National League player in the 1960s?

22. What player has received the highest percentage of Hall of Fame votes in baseball history?

23. Who holds the record for home runs in a two-year period?

24. Who holds the record for home runs in a five-year period?

25. Who holds the record for home runs in a ten-year period?

26. Who holds the record for home runs in a fifteen-year period?

27. Who holds the record for home runs in a twenty-year period?

28. Who holds the American League record for home runs in a season?

29. What pitcher had the greatest single-year winning percentage in the twentieth century for a season with twenty or more victories?

30. What American League team scored the most runs in one season?

31. What National League team scored the most runs in one season?

32. What American League team hit the most home runs in one season?

33. What National League team hit the most home runs in one season?

34. What American League team had the most 20-game winners in one season?

35. Who had the lowest single-season ERA in the twentieth century?

36. Name the four Major League catchers with more than 300 homers.

37. What American League hurler was the first 30-game winner of the twentieth century?

38. Babe Ruth was the first player to reach 500 home runs. Who was the second?

39. What National League pitchers were the first 30-game winners of the twentieth century?

40. This slugger holds the Major League record for leading his league in home runs the most times.

41. This slugger holds the record for most 100-run seasons.

42. He had more 200-hit seasons than any player in baseball history.

43. This specialist is the all-time leader in pinch hits.

44. This player is the all-time leader in singles.

45. This stalwart defensive outfielder is also the all-time leader in doubles.

46. If it's triples you want, this outfielder is still the all-time leader.

47. He still has more home runs than any switch-hitter in baseball history.

48. The 1963 Cardinals had three players with 200 or more hits. Who were they?

49. He had more multiple home run games than any other hitter.

50. Name the five players (playing 1,000 or more games) with career slugging averages above .600.

51. Name the all-time leader in drawing walks.

52. There are five players in baseball history have 800 stolen bases. Name four.

53. Name the two players who are tied for most 50-steal seasons.

54. He started more games, completed more games, and won more games than any pitcher in baseball history.

55. What 300-game winner had a record twenty 200-inning seasons?

56. This pitcher had a record sixteen 300-inning seasons.

57. This right-hander had sixteen 20-win seasons.

58. After not winning his first game until he was twenty-five, this pitcher had thirteen 20-win seasons.

59. What right-hander is the all-time leader in saves?

60. This Hall of Famer won 266 games despite losing nearly four complete years (from ages twenty-three to twenty-six) to World War II.

61. He is the all-time leader with 110 shutouts.

62. These two power-pitching right-handers each threw 12 one-hitters.

63. In the last fifty-five years, only three men have pitched 350 or more innings in a season. Name two of them.

64. This pitcher walked more batters, threw more wild pitches, and lost more games than any pitcher of the twentieth century.

65. At the age of twenty-three, this shortstop became only the third player ever to get 40 homers and 40 steals in the same season.

66. He became the first player in Major League history to hit 400 home runs and steal 400 bases.

67. Who was the first player in Major League history to hit 50 homers in consecutive seasons?

68. He is the only pitcher in baseball history to win the Cy Young Award five times.

69. He was the first player ever to have 50 homers and 50 doubles in the same season.

70. Who are the three catchers in the 2,000-games-caught club?

71. Who broke Don Drysdale's record for consecutive scoreless innings?

72. How many hits did Ty Cobb have?

73. What two National League pitchers combined for 6 consecutive strikeouts in the 1984 All-Star Game?

74. What did Ted Williams do to ensure his .400 average in 1941?

75. Who had 20 doubles, 20 triples, and 20 homers in the 1941 season?

76. After Jeff Heath turned the feat, who was the next to do it?

1. Carl Yastrzemski and Brooks Robinson

2. Nolan Ryan, with twenty-seven; Tommy John, with twenty-six; Charlie Hough, with twenty-five; Jim Kaat, with twenty-five

3. Walter Johnson, with the Senators; Ted Lyons, with the White Sox

4. Pete Rose, with 3,562

5. 2,632 games

6. Ty Cobb, with .366; Rogers Hornsby, with .358; Joe Jackson, with .356

7. Frank Howard

8. Honus Wagner and Tony Gwynn both led eight times.

9. Ty Cobb

10. Buddy Bell, Dave Concepcion, Dave Parker, Tony Perez, Pete Rose

11. Pete Rose, with 14,053

12. Steve Garvey, with 1,207

13. The Boston Pilgrims beat Pittsburgh, 5 games to 3, in 1903.

14. The New York Yankees have won twenty-six.

15. The New York Yankees have won eight World Series since 1961.

16. Willie Stargell, with 296

17. False. After Hornsby won the batting title in 1928, Lefty O'Doul hit .398 in 1929.

18. Babe Ruth, Lou Gehrig, Jimmie Foxx, Ted Williams, Henry Aaron

19. False. Bill Terry hit .401 in 1930.

20. Steve Carlton threw 304 innings in 1980.

21. Roberto Clemente batted .328 for the decade.

22. Tom Seaver

23. Mark McGwire hit 135 home runs in 1998 and 1999.

24. Mark McGwire, with 284 from 1995 through 1999

25. Babe Ruth, with 467 from 1920 through 1929

26. Babe Ruth, with 660 from 1919 through 1933

27. Hank Aaron hit 713 from 1954 through 1973.

28. Roger Maris, with 61

29. Ron Guidry. He was 25–3 in 1978 for a percentage of .893.

30. The 1931 New York Yankees scored 1,067 runs (6.97 per game).

31. The Cardinals scored 1,004 runs in 1930.

32. Seattle hit 264 home runs in 1997.

33. The 1997 Rockies hit 239 home runs. Before that, the 1947 Giants and 1956 Reds, each with 221 homers, held the record. The 1998 Cardinals had 223 homers.

34. The 1971 Orioles had four 20-game winners: Dave McNally, with 21; Mike Cuellar, with 20; Pat Dobson, with 20; Jim Palmer, with 20. As did the 1920 Chicago White Sox with Red Faber, with 23; Lefty Williams, with 22; Eddie Cicotte, with 21; Dickie Kerr, with 21

35. Dutch Leonard, in 1914, with a 0.96 ERA

36. Johnny Bench, with 389; Carlton Fisk, with 376; Yogi Berra, with 358; Gary Carter, with 324

37. Cy Young won 33 for Boston in 1901.

38. Jimmie Foxx

39. Joe McGinnity won 31 and Christy Mathewson won 30 for the Giants in 1903.

40. Ruth led the American League in home runs 12 times.

41. Hank Aaron scored 100 or more runs 15 times.

42. Pete Rose had ten 200-hit seasons.

43. Manny Mota had 150 pinch hits.

44. Pete Rose had 3,215 singles.

45. Tris Speaker had 792 doubles.

46. Sam Crawford had 309 triples.

47. Mickey Mantle hit 536 home runs.

48. Dick Groat, with 201; Curt Flood, with 200; Bill White, with 200

49. Babe Ruth had 72 multiple home run games.

50. Babe Ruth, with .690; Ted Williams, with .634; Lou Gehrig, with .632; Jimmie Foxx, with .609; Hank Greenberg, with .605

51. Rickey Henderson, with 2,060.

52. Rickey Henderson, with 1,334; Lou Brock, with 938; Billy Hamilton, with 912; Ty Cobb, with 892; Tim Raines, with 807

53. Rickey Henderson and Lou Brock

54. Cy Young

55. Don Sutton

56. Cy Young

57. Cy Young

58. Warren Spahn

59. Lee Smith saved 478 games.

60. Bob Feller

61. Walter Johnson

62. Bob Feller and Nolan Ryan

63. Wilbur Wood of the White Sox had 377 in 1972 and 359 in 1973; Mickey Lolich of the Tigers had 376 in 1971; and Bob Feller of the Indians had 371 in 1946.

64. Nolan Ryan

65. Alex Rodriguez

66. Barry Bonds

67. Babe Ruth, in 1920 with 54 and 1921 with 59. He repeated the feat in 1927 with 60 and 1928 with 54.

68. Roger Clemens

69. Albert Belle

70. Bob Boone, Gary Carter, Carlton Fisk

71. Orel Hershiser threw 59 consecutive scoreless innings in 1988.

72. Ty Cobb is currently credited with 4,189 hits. In 1981 it was discovered that Cobb was credited twice for the same two-hit game. Thus two hits were removed from his total.

73. Fernando Valenzuela and Dwight Gooden. Valenzuela fanned Dave Winfield, Reggie Jackson, and George Brett in the fourth inning, and Gooden fanned Lance Parrish, Chet Lemon, and Alvin Davis in the fifth.

74. In a doubleheader on September 28, 1941, Williams had the option of sitting out and finishing the season at .400. Instead, he played both ends of the doubleheader, and went 4 for 5 in the first game and 2 for 3 in the second game to finish at .406.

75. Jeff Heath hit 32 doubles, 20 triples, and 24 home runs for the Cleveland Indians.

76. In 1957 Willie Mays had 26 doubles, 20 triples, and 35 homers.

CHAPTER 6

The World Series

1. True or false: There have been no 4-game sweeps in the World Series since 1975 that didn't involve a New York team.

2. Who was the first black pitcher to appear in a World Series?

3. Name the two players who have hit 3 home runs in a World Series game.

4. Who is the player who has hit the most home runs in a single World Series?

5. What pitcher has thrown the most shutouts in a single World Series?

6. What pitcher has won the most World Series games?

7. Who has won the most World Series games without losing?

8. What is the team record for consecutive World Series games won?

9. What is the team record for consecutive years winning the World Series?

10. Which teams are second and third in most World Championships won?

11. What National League team was the first ever to win consecutive World Series?

12. What American League team was the first to win consecutive World Series?

13. Who are the two mangers tied with seven World Series won?

14. Which two players hit .418 for the highest averages in World Series history in 13 or more games?

15. Who is the leader with seven World Series saves?

16. Who is the all-time leader in World Series games, at bats, hits, and doubles?

17. Who is the all-time leader in World Series home runs?

18. Who has the lowest ERA of any American League hurler in World Series history (with a minimum of thirty innings pitched)?

19. Who has the lowest ERA of any National League hurler in World Series history (with a minimum of thirty innings pitched)?

20. How many home runs were hit in the game where Babe Ruth allegedly called his shot?

1. False. The Oakland A's swept the San Francisco Giants in 1989, and the Cincinnati Reds swept the Oakland A's in the 1990 World Series.

2. Satchel Paige, who appeared in Game Five of the 1948 Series for Cleveland

3. Babe Ruth and Reggie Jackson

4. Reggie Jackson. He hit five in the 1977 World Series.

5. Christy Mathewson. He hurled 3 shutouts in the 1905 World Series.

6. Whitey Ford won ten.

7. Lefty Gomez won six World Series games from 1932 through 1938.

8. The Yankees won the last four games of the 1996 Series, swept the 1998 and 1999 Series, and won the first two games of the 2000 Series.

9. Five. The Yankees won each fall classic from 1949 through 1953.

10. The Athletics (of Philadelphia and Oakland) have won nine World Series, as have the St. Louis Cardinals. The Dodgers are fourth with six World Series won.

11. The Chicago Cubs, in 1907 and 1908

12. The Philadelphia Athletics, in 1910 and 1911

13. Joe McCarthy and Casey Stengel

14. Pepper Martin and Paul Molitor both hit .418 in World Series play.

15. Mariano Rivera

16. Yogi Berra (tied in doubles with Frankie Frisch)

17. Mickey Mantle, with 18

18. Babe Ruth owns a 0.87 ERA in World Series play.

19. Harry Brecheen has an 0.83 World Series ERA.

20. 5. Babe Ruth and Lou Gehrig each hit 2 for the Yankees and Gabby Hartnett hit 1 for the Cubs.

CHAPTER 7

Awards and Honors

1. Name the first five players to be elected to the Baseball Hall of Fame.

2. From 1931 through 1933 the American League MVP award was won by players on the Philadelphia A's. Who were they?

3. This 1950 MVP led the Major League in sacrifices in four consecutive years.

4. True or false: Stan Musial won four MVP awards.

5. Who was the first Yankee to win the home run championship?

6. Who was the first Tiger to win an MVP award?

7. What three Hall of Famers played during the 1970s and never played a day in the minor leagues?

8. In the 1950s, the San Francisco Giants had first basemen win the Rookie of the Year Award in consecutive seasons. Name these two players—both of whom later won MVP awards.

9. Who was the first American Leaguer to win the Cy Young Award?

10. There are two players eligible for, but not yet in, the Hall of Fame who won back-to-back MVPs. Who are they?

11. Who were the last two players to win a Triple Crown and an MVP in the same season?

12. Who was the first New York Yankees player to win an MVP award?

13. When was the last season two players shared an MVP award?

14. Who were the Cy Young Award winners in 1967, the first year that one award was given in each league?

15. Who was the first player from the Negro Leagues to be elected to the Hall of Fame?

16. Since 1950, only two Phillies have won MVP awards. Who are they?

17. Who was the first black player to win a batting title?

18. From 1960 to 1982, twenty-five All-Star Games were played. How many did the American League win?

19. What National League pitcher led the league in wins from 1957 through 1961?

20. Who was the first player ever to win the World Series MVP award twice?

21. Who was the most recent player to win the World Series MVP award twice?

22. Who was the other player, this one a pitcher, to win the World Series MVP award twice?

23. He won more Gold Gloves than any other first baseman.

24. This Pittsburgh infielder is often regarded as the greatest defensive second baseman of all time and won eight Gold Glove Awards.

25. This onetime National League MVP finished second in the nation in scoring in college basketball during the 1951–1952 season.

26. The 1937 Tigers had four 200-hit players. Name three of them.

27. At shortstop this National Leaguer captured thirteen Gold Gloves.

28. Two outfielders have twelve Gold Gloves. Name them.

29. This Cleveland second baseman has won nine Gold Gloves.

30. Name the two American League outfielders who won ten Gold Gloves each.

1. In 1936, Ty Cobb, Walter Johnson, Christy Mathewson, Babe Ruth, and Honus Wagner were elected.

2. Lefty Grove, in 1931; Jimmie Foxx, in 1932, 1933

3. Phil Rizzuto, from 1949 through 1952

4. False. He won the award three times, in 1943, 1946, and 1948.

5. Wally Pipp led in 1916 and 1917.

6. Ty Cobb, in 1911

7. Ernie Banks, Catfish Hunter, Al Kaline

8. Orlando Cepeda in 1958; Willie McCovey in 1959

9. Bob Turley in 1958

10. Dale Murphy and Roger Maris

11. Frank Robinson, in 1966; Carl Yastrzemski, in 1967

12. Babe Ruth, in 1923

13. In 1979 Keith Hernandez and Willie Stargell shared the MVP award.

14. Mike McCormick, with San Francisco, and Jim Lonborg, with Boston

15. Jackie Robinson, in 1962

16. Jim Konstanty, in 1950, and Mike Schmidt, in 1980, 1981, 1986

17. Jackie Robinson, in 1949

18. Two: in 1962 and 1971

19. Warren Spahn

20. Sandy Koufax, in 1963 and 1965

21. Reggie Jackson won the award in 1973 and 1977.

22. Bob Gibson, in 1964 and 1967

23. Keith Hernandez won the award eleven times, every year from 1978 through 1988.

24. Bill Mazeroski

25. Dick Groat, who played basketball for Duke

26. Gee Walker, with 213; Charlie Gehringer, with 209; Pete Fox, with 208; Hank Greenberg, with 200.

27. Ozzie Smith won the award every year from 1980 through 1992.

28. Willie Mays, in 1957–1968, and Roberto Clemente, in 1961–1972

29. Roberto Alomar

30. Al Kaline, in 1957–1959 and 1961–1967, and Ken Griffey, Jr., in 1990–1999.

CHAPTER 8

Nicknames

1. How did George Herman Ruth get the nickname "Babe"?

2. He was called "the Babe Ruth of the Negro Leagues."

3. He was known as "the Barber."

4. This RBI king was known as "Doggie."

5. This turn-of-the-century star was known as "Big Ed."

6. Who was called "Big Six"?

7. Name the hurler known as "the Big Train."

8. Who was known as "the Bird"?

9. Elston Howard called him "the Chairman of the Board."

10. This Hall of Famer was dubbed "the Commerce Comet."

11. This speedster was called "Cool Papa."

12. Who was "the Dominican Dandy"?

13. This Hall of Fame hurler was known as "the Franchise."

14. What second baseman was known as "the Fordham Flash"?

15. Who was "the Grey Eagle"?

16. He led the league in homers four times and was known as "Home Run."

17. Who was "the Junk Man"?

18. Who was "the Little Napoleon"?

19. "The Little Professor" was this outfielder's moniker.

20. "Louisiana Lightning" was this left-hander's label.

21. What lefty hitter was called "Master Melvin"?

22. He earned the name "Mr. October."

23. Who was "Nap"?

24. Baseball's greatest hypochondriac was called "Old Aches and Pains."

25. "Old Pete" was a storied hurler.

26. "Pie" was this infielder's sobriquet.

27. This team leader was known as "Pops."

28. This recent Hall of Famer's affectionate nickname was "Pudge."

The Major League Baseball Book of Fabulous Facts and Awesome Trivia

29. This infielder was called "Rabbit."

30. They called this outfielder "the Say Hey Kid."

31. Who was "Sudden Sam"?

32. This legend was known as "the Splendid Splinter."

33. Who was "Stretch"?

34. "The Sultan of Swat" was just one of his nicknames.

35. This hurler was known as "Three Finger."

1. When Baltimore manager Jack Dunn introduced the nineteen-year-old Ruth to his teammates in 1914, one remarked, "Boys, here's Jack's new Babe."

2. Josh Gibson (1912–1947), reported to have hit 72 homers in one year.

3. Sal Maglie got the name for "shaving batters" with inside pitches.

4. Tony Perez got this tag for driving in so many runs.

5. The Philadelphia outfielder Ed Delehanty was six feet and 170 pounds and hit .346 for his career.

6. Christy Mathewson

7. Walter Johnson

8. Mark Fidrych

9. Whitey Ford

10. Mickey Mantle

11. James "Cool Papa" Bell was an outfielder with legendary speed.

12. Juan Marichal

13. Tom Seaver

14. Frankie Frisch

15. Tris Speaker

16. John Franklin Baker, who led the league in homers from 1911 through 1914

17. Eddie Lopat, who many said pitched with three speeds—slow, slower, and stop

18. John McGraw, the smallish Giants manager who was an unyielding leader of his teams

19. Dom DiMaggio, the Boston outfielder who cut a bookish appearance in his wire-rimmed glasses

20. Ron Guidry, who despite his lean frame threw hard

21. Mel Ott, for his ability to hit home runs down the short right-field line at the Polo Grounds

22. Reggie Jackson

23. Hall of Fame second baseman Napoleon Lajoie

24. Luke Appling, who complained about an unending array of injuries, some real but most imagined

25. Grover Cleveland Alexander

26. Third baseman Harold Traynor got this nickname for helping to shag balls for the Sommerville, Massachusetts, team that he was too young to play for. When a priest, Father Nangle, would take him to a grocery store for his reward, he usually said, "I'll take pie."

27. Willie Stargell

28. Carlton Fisk

29. Walter "Rabbit" Maranville was a rangy infielder and fast base runner.

30. Willie Mays, who when he forgot someone's name would say, "Uh, say hey."

31. Sam McDowell, who threw with great velocity

32. Ted Williams, because he was tall and incredibly thin

33. At 6 feet, 4 inches, Willie McCovey presented a big target at first base and could reach most any throw.

34. Babe Ruth got this nickname from baseball "poet" Franklin P. Adams:

> *Babe Ruth and Old Jack Dempsey*
> *Both Sultans of Swat,*
> *One hits where other people are—*
> *The other where they're not.*

35. As a youngster, Mordecai Peter Centennial Brown got his right hand caught in a corn shredder, cutting off one finger and mangling another.

CHAPTER 9

Extra Innings

1. What was Babe Ruth's career record as a pitcher?

2. Name the two players who stole 100 or more bases in two different seasons.

3. Who is the only player to homer in every game of a League Championship Series?

4. Who is the last player to lead both leagues in stolen bases?

5. Name four players with ten or more letters in their last names who hit 40 or more homers in a season.

6. Who are the seven Hall of Famers whose last names are the same as United States presidents' names?

7. He set a rookie record when he stole 72 bases.

8. What reliever won an American League record 17 games in his rookie season?

9. He pitched in sixty-five 1–0 games, winning 38 and losing 27 of them. In 20 of his 1–0 losses he allowed 4 or fewer hits.

10. He hit .382 (with 570 at bats) in his last year in the Major Leagues.

11. Who was the first switch-hitter to win a batting title?

12. Who is the most recent Cub to win 20 or more games six years in a row?

13. Who was the only player to hit 4 homers in two different World Series?

14. Name the player who batted .322 and ended his career with 2,987 hits.

15. Who was the only catcher to win two batting crowns?

16. Who became the first pitcher since Jim Palmer (1975 to 1978) to win 20 or more games for four consecutive seasons?

17. Who was the youngest player to hit 50 homers in a season?

18. He had 40 homers by the end of July 1994 to set a league mark.

19. This National Leaguer hit 35 homers in his rookie year, second only to Wally Berger's 38 with the Boston Braves in 1930 and Frank Robinson's 38 with Cincinnati in 1956.

20. Who was the first player in history to be selected to the All-Star team as catcher and then at second base?

21. Whose 1.56 ERA in 1994 was 1.09 lower than the ERA of the next-lowest Major League hurler?

22. Name the third sacker who hit .300 for eight consecutive years (1946–1953) in the American League.

The Major League Baseball Book of Fabulous Facts and Awesome Trivia

23. He is the only outfielder to play in 1,000 or more consecutive games.

24. Name the four Dodgers who hit 30 or more homers in 1977.

25. He hit a record 9 home runs in three consecutive World Series.

1. 94–46, with a 2.26 ERA

2. Vince Coleman and Rickey Henderson

3. Hank Aaron, in 1969

4. Ron LeFlore, who stole 68 with Detroit in 1978 and 97 with Montreal in 1980

5. Ted Kluszewski, in 1953 and 1954; Roy Campanella, in 1953; Carl Yastrzemski, in 1967; Rico Petrocelli, in 1969

6. Walter, Ban, and Judy Johnson; Reggie and Travis Jackson; Hack Wilson; Whitey Ford

7. Juan Samuel, in 1984

8. Bill Campbell, in 1976, with the Twins

9. Walter Johnson

10. Joe Jackson

11. Mickey Mantle, in 1956

12. Ferguson Jenkins, from 1967 through 1972

13. Duke Snider, in 1952 and 1955

14. Sam Rice

15. Ernie Lombardi, with the 1936 Reds and the 1942 Boston Braves

16. Dave Stewart, in 1987–1990 for Oakland

17. Willie Mays, who was twenty-four with the 1955 Giants

18. Matt Williams, for San Francisco

19. Mike Piazza, in 1993

20. Craig Biggio, in 1991 and 1992

21. Greg Maddux

22. George Kell

23. Billy Williams

24. Steve Garvey, with 33; Reggie Smith, with 32; Ron Cey, with 30; Dusty Baker, with 30

25. Babe Ruth, who hit 4 in 1926, 2 in 1927, 3 in 1928

Bibliography

Forker, Dom. *The Ultimate Baseball Quiz Book*. New York: Signet, 1988.

Losano, Wayne A. *Official Major League Baseball Fact Book*, 2000 edition. St. Louis: Sporting News, 2000.

Murphy, John. *The Bathroom Baseball Book*. Saddle River, NJ: Red-Letter Press, 1988.

Palmer, Pete, and Thorn, John. *Total Baseball*, 6th edition. New York: Total Sports Publishing, 1999.

Shouler, Kenneth. *The Real 100 Best Players of All-Time and Why*. Lenexa, KS: Addax Publishing, 1998.

Acknowledgments

Special thanks to the boys at Runyon's whose appetite for trivia was every bit as great as it was for the items on the menu. Thanks also to SABR members Clifford Blau and Peter Hassell, who have unearthed and donated a few good questions. Appreciation to Don Hintze at Major League Baseball, Eric Enders at the Hall of Fame, and Matthew Benjamin at HarperCollins, who all reviewed the manuscript.

Photo Credits

KEN SHOULER is senior editor of reference at Total Sports Publishing. He was one of the panelists selected by Major League Baseball to pick the "All-Century Team" in 1999 and appeared in MLB's All-Century video. His books include *The Real 100 Best Baseball Players of All-Time and Why* and *The Experts Pick Basketball's Best 50 Players in the Last 50 Years*. He is currently a writer and project editor for two encyclopedias, *Total Basketball* and *Total Billiards: The World Encyclopedia of Cue Sports*. He is also project editor for *Total Boxing*. Before joining Total Sports Publishing he taught philosophy for eighteen years at the City University of New York and freelanced for many magazines, including *Sport, Inside Sports, Arts and Entertainment, Biography*, and several *Street and Smith's* annuals. He writes regularly for *Cigar Aficionado* and lives in Harrison, New York, with his wife, Rose Marie.